D1048820

Do Fly

Find your way.
Make a living.
Be your best self.

Gavin Strange

CHRONICLE BOOKS
SAN FRANCISCO

First published in the United States of
America in 2018 by Chronicle Books LLC.

Originally published in the
United Kingdom in 2016 by
The Do Book Company.

Copyright © 2016 by Gavin Strange.

Photograph on page 120 copyright
© 2016 by Curtis James.

All rights reserved. No part of this
book may be reproduced in any form without
written permission from the publisher.

Library of Congress Cataloging-
in-Publication Data available.

ISBN: 978-1-4521-7147-0

Manufactured in China.

MIX
Paper from
responsible sources
FSC™ C136333
FSC
www.fsc.org

Cover design by James Victore.
Book illustrated, designed, and set
by JamFactory and Ratiotype.

Photography by Gavin Strange. Shot
on Kodak Portra film, with a Leica
M6 and 50mm Summicron lens.

10 9 8 7 6 5 4 3 2 1

Chronicle Books LLC
680 Second Street
San Francisco, California 94107

www.chroniclebooks.com

For Janey

For Sully

For Mum and Dad

For Dan

CONTENTS

Hello there! Let me offer you a warm welcome to *Do Fly*.

Is your seat comfortable? Good. Do you have a refreshing beverage in hand? Smashing. Then shall we begin our journey? Fantastic.

This book that you're holding in your hands will be your all-in-one guide, ticket, and passport to your new destination. Where exactly are we going? Well, I'm not sure, that's for you to decide . . .

We can arouse your curiosity to discover a new hobby or set you on a path to a brand-new career. Maybe this is your first time flying solo, and the choice of places to visit or paths to follow is overwhelming—fear not; I'm here to help guide you.

What I'm getting at in this ridiculously metaphor-laden introduction is about you, the lovely reader, going on a "journey" (sorry for the *X-Factor* lingo), finding what you love, and making that your focus. Your ultimate goal is to blend what you enjoy doing and what you get paid to do, so they're one and the same!

Madness, right!? Work is "work," and the fun stuff comes once you've left for the day. Nope, it doesn't have to be. It's totally possible to find or create a job you love that encapsulates all your passions and interests. It's also totally possible to find a new vocation, do a total 180-degree turn, and start afresh. It sounds mythical because that's what "other people" do. We've all read stories or seen articles where some clever so-and-so gives up their successful job in accounting to become a baker and lives happily ever after. Well, yes, that does happen to other people, but it can happen to you, too.

You just have to DO it, and that's what this book is all about—encouraging you, pushing you, and, most importantly, reminding you that life's too short not to pursue the goals you want to achieve, whatever your age or position. You might be a CEO or a college student. It doesn't matter. We all deserve the chance to discover and fight to do the things that make us happy.

I'm not saying any of this is easy. What follows comes with a load of caveats. But if it was easy, it wouldn't seem so magical to have work and play fuse together and for us to find a job at the intersection of where these two things meet.

But it's also about going beyond that. You might already have your dream job, but that fills up only eight hours a day, right? What are you going to do for the rest of the night?

Well, let me introduce my good friend, the side project. This is a great way to try new things and discover new places that may influence your work and ultimately even change your final destination. So we'll be making a lot of regular stops on this flight, to refuel and to give you a chance to stretch your legs.

Be patient though. Finding your way, making a living, and being your best self is a never-ending pursuit. There's always something new to learn, a new goal to be achieved. What you think you already know can change in the blink of an eye and make you reassess everything—but that's a wonderful thing!

The creative path to happiness takes a different route for everyone, but traveling together is a lot more fun! So let's do this thing.

I hope that what you find in these pages helps you, guides you, makes you chuckle, makes you think, and, most importantly, makes you happy. Because, after all, as rapper and musician Ghostpoet sang:

"LIFE'S TOO SHORT TO STORE OUR GRUDGES. LIFE'S TOO LONG TO MAKE NO PLANS."

So, without further ado, I'm going to ask you to please stow away your tray tables, turn off your cell phones, fasten your seat belts, and prepare for takeoff.

Now we're on the runway; it's time to get down to business!

I want to kick things off by positively changing the way we look at "work" because it should be something that excites us, not depresses us! While growing up, work can be seen as the end of being childlike, the beginning of being an adult, and a place where fun is strictly outlawed. I'm not sure where this comes from, as I don't think it has ever been said out loud. But it's certainly assumed.

This notion that work should be endured, that it is drudgery, is madness. It doesn't have to be! Now, there's a huge caveat here. There are loads of jobs out there that are laborious and downright difficult, and I like to refer to that as "real work." And thank goodness there are some mighty fine people who are good at that stuff. So this section should really be called "Work *can* be enjoyed, not endured."

If, like me, you are lucky enough to work in a sector that requires creative thinking (and that's a massive scope of jobs) or want to get into the creative industries, then don't look at work as a necessity—think of it as an opportunity.

This might sound like I'm singling out the arts right away and elevating it. But a "creative" job isn't limited to artists, designers, and people who enjoy coloring books. No way. Creativity is used everywhere. It's problem solving—using knowledge, intuition, and ingenuity to reach a desired outcome. So that includes pretty much every kind of job ever then, right? Nice!

Ultimately, you need to adopt the right mindset. Try and put salary to one side for a minute. What if you look at work as a challenge, as a game, as a way to get ahead? Most of us will spend a huge proportion of our lives working, so we should do something we enjoy, find interesting and engaging. It's an opportunity to change things, mold things, make things, break things, and be downright disruptive.

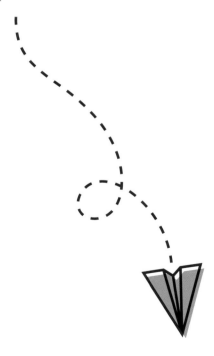

DON'T HAVE ALL THE ANSWERS

• • • • • •

Answers. Who has them? Grown-ups, apparently. When we're kids, we live in this blissful world of Lego, endless bike rides, Thomas the Tank Engine, and [insert your own childhood obsessions here]. It's a world free of any responsibility.

This continues for years and years. More Lego, more bike rides, more Thomas the Tank Engine (naturally progressing to Mutant Ninja Turtles, of course). It's wonderful, a seemingly never-ending state of "play."

Play without thought or reason. And then it comes: the Question.

"What do you want to be when you grow up?"

At first it's an innocent little question. So inevitably you blurt out whatever you're obsessed with at the time.

"A Mutant Ninja Turtle!" you reply.

They tolerate that response for a little while, but there's only so many times you can give the answer of wanting to be a genetically altered reptile with a knowledge of martial arts.

The question becomes more and more frequent over the years, until you realize they want an answer. A proper answer. A satisfactory answer. The thing is, you're fifteen years old—how can you possibly know? There's a lot going on when you're in your teens, so being asked what you want to do for the next fifty years is, quite understandably, terrifying.

Some people have a clear idea of what they want to do from a very young age. They have that drive and vision. They seem to inherently know what their life's work will be. And that's very cool, and if you have that, then you're lucky. But I'm sure I wasn't alone in being totally clueless when asked such a big question at such a young age.

But guess what? It's okay to not have all the answers. That's not to say you shouldn't have thoughts and ideas about what you'd like to do in your life, but you need time to discover the things you love and find interesting. These discoveries may one day form into a neat, concise answer of: "I want to do *that!*"

This doesn't apply only to high-school or college graduates either. The pressure gets even greater as you get older. Once you have a "job," many of us can find it's easier to stay in it, working our way up the ladder. There is an expectation that we'll stay: "Well, you chose to be here; why would you go anywhere else?"

No way! You are in control of your career and your personal happiness. You need to make sure you are spending your time and energy on the things you care about. Sure, that's idealistic! But why would you not want to live in an ideal world?

WE ARE ALL BORN FREE, WE DIE BY THE SHACKLES WE ADOPT. ENJOY YOUR BUOYANCY, RIGHT UP UNTIL THE VERY LAST DROP.

Sage Francis, "Dead Man's Float"

From the outset, we feel we're in control of what we do, but as time goes on, it can be very easy to get "shackled" to things or a way of life we don't necessarily want to lead.

It's not an easy process. This is a lifelong challenge of following your own intuition and interests, directing yourself toward the good things—and steering yourself away from those not so good—all the while being open and honest, connecting with others, and collaborating. This first stage of learning to fly is about asking those questions and finding the right answers. Maybe you already have the right one.

So instead of asking, "What do I want to be when I grow up?"maybe reframe the question for yourself and consider, "What kind of person do I want to be when I grow up?"

TIME FOR A CHANGE

Change can mean different things to different people. It can be exciting, terrifying, something to be feared, or something to be embraced. But the truth is, we all need to be open to the idea of change.

To move forward, something usually has to change. It could be as simple as swapping what kind of pencil you use or as profound as altering your whole belief system. No matter what the scale of change is, all changes are valid, as it means you're starting to consider other possibilities or other ways of doing things.

Sometimes the hardest part can be realizing and then accepting that things need to change. It's hard because it's scary. Really scary. Having comfort in our routine is lovely. It's . . . it's . . . comfortable, and that's a wonderful feeling. To suddenly disrupt that feels crazy, but sometimes it has to be done to get to a better place. Think of it as a bit of turbulence. Trust me; it'll soon pass, and then you'll be above the clouds!

So, you want to change things? You want something new? Good. Good! If you're in a rut, I'm not going to help you get out. I'm going to *show* you how to get out of it yourself.

BE THE CHANGE YOU WANT TO SEE

● ● ● ● ● ●

Obviously this book is being super-idealistic and all these nice floaty sentiments about just doing what you love, blah, blah, are annoying, right? Well, maybe I am an idealist.

It's so easy to get eaten up by cynicism and negativity, thinking that the good stuff doesn't happen to people like you, and the opportunities just don't present themselves. So start by redirecting some of your time and energy to change that. Start bridging gaps, start conversations, start sowing seeds. Don't focus on what isn't happening; focus on what could happen.

If you don't feel there's a group that represents you—start one that does. If there's something missing from the conversation—introduce that missing piece.

If you're working within a larger organization, you'll have to find the boundaries of what you can and can't change. Push gently against the things you'd like to be different, help and encourage others with things you'd like to see change. I'm not advocating a hostile or aggressive position, totally the opposite—you can make changes by being a kind, warm, and passionate person.

My friend and fellow speaker at the Do Lectures, Sarah Corbett, founded the "Craftivist Collective," which combines craft (usually in the form of cross-stitching) and activism to engage people in social change. She does this respectfully and peacefully as "gentle activism." And it works. A few years ago, Sarah was constantly pestering her local member of parliament—sending petitions and forwarding on issues—so much so that the MP told her to stop, saying, "It's a waste of your time and my time." Obviously frustrated with such a response, Sarah knew she had to appeal to the MP in a different way, so she decided to provoke rather than preach. She used her craft skills to make the MP a handkerchief, embroidered with a personal message and the line, "Don't blow it!"

This personal touch led to Sarah meeting with the MP; they sat down and talked with each other, rather than at each other. They now have an ongoing relationship of "critical friendship"—the MP uses her powers to help those who most need it, guided by Sarah, and in return the MP helps Sarah with how best to use her own skills as an activist.

It's proof that to make changes you don't have to be an extrovert or a lunatic; you just have to have drive and purpose. How you manifest that drive is up to you— there's no right or wrong way.

And things will naturally change, too. So you'll have to constantly reevaluate yourself. What you want and need from your work and personal life can and will change often. So be sure to take time out every now and then to take stock of what you're thinking and feeling.

In practical terms, you can do that by just stepping outside of your normal routine—disrupt your schedule a little and give yourself a bit of time to reflect. Make a mental note to check in with yourself regularly. It could be as grand as scheduling a mini-holiday to take some time off and assess your life and work. Try and go away on your own—radical, eh? Or it could be as simple as using a train journey to switch off the social media and just contemplate. Are you happy? Are you being the change you want to see? Ask yourself these questions.

As much as this is an individual pursuit, do take a look at what other people need, too. Do your ideas and goals line up with what your colleagues and comrades are doing? Do you believe there's a better way to do something that will benefit everyone? Collaborating with others to make change happen can bring it about much quicker, so seek out those positive souls who share your desire for change.

Communication is also key for those who don't want change. Opposition exists in organizations of every shape and size, so being able to passionately relay your desire for making things different is essential. Sarah's Craftivist manifesto point, "Provoke Don't Preach," fits perfectly with this—encourage discussion and new points of view; don't force it. Force is often met with resistance.

Change? It's suddenly sounding like a long tightrope to walk, isn't it? It sure as hell won't be easy, but it'll be worth it. You want to get to the other side, right?

SEEK CREATIVE SATISFACTION
WHEREVER YOU CAN GET IT

• • • • • •

Now I know I just said, "Be the change," and told you to go and make everything better, but I also know that in reality this can be really hard. Chances are you'll hit a big corporate-size brick wall. So, if you simply can't improve things during the day, what about doing it at night? Stealth mode!

One thing I've learned is that time is one of the greatest levelers. No matter how much money, power, or advantage you have, each of us has only twenty-four hours in the day, and that will never change. So use that time wisely. Think of it like a currency and spend it as best you can.

Go home after work, say hello to your loved ones, make some dinner, and then get cracking with something that makes you happy. Seek that satisfaction in the wee hours; look for it in places you don't expect. The television set is a wonderful invention, but it's also a time vortex that'll suck your life away. Keep your eye on the clock and get busy doing the things you want to do. There's no amount of

Breaking Bad that can bring you eternal happiness. (Sorry, Mr. Cranston.)

Start small—that really helps. After a long, difficult day, it can be incredibly hard to summon the energy needed to start actively engaging your brain again, especially as the night draws in. So set yourself a little target—something realistic and achievable. Maybe once a week set aside an hour to practice a new skill or indulge in a hobby. Then try twice a week, maybe doubling the time you allow. It's really hard to imagine delving into more "work" when you're feeling tired, but as soon as you discover the feeling of satisfaction and pride once you've completed one small task, you'll be back for more.

Find a routine that works for you. Everyone's different, and it will depend on which extracurricular activities you choose as to how and when you'll best fit them in. When it came to writing this book, I needed to find a new routine. I couldn't seem to write in the evenings, so I'd get up an hour earlier each day before work to get creative! It was really difficult some mornings, but once I had a coffee by my side and some gentle music playing, I could get in the zone. The first day I did this, the feeling I had once I realized I'd accomplished something before 8 a.m.—before work!— was wonderful. After that, there was no stopping me. And the fact that you now have a finished book in your hands means that it paid off!

Find the pattern that suits you. Find the rhythm that feels right. Keep it manageable. This could be as simple as finding and following a new group of people on Instagram or Twitter who all do things you'd like to do. Or see if that website domain name you like is still available. Before you know it, you'll be more productive than you ever thought you could be!

MONEY VS. HAPPINESS

• • • • • •

Now then, this is a tricky one: Do you do what pays well or what makes you happy?

Well, this book strictly operates within the inspirational and positive world of idealism, so I'm going to convince you to go with what makes you happy. Actually, on one level, it's really easy to do what makes you happy—you follow and pursue what makes your heart sing. The hard part is taking that passion and getting someone to pay you for it! But it's by no means impossible.

Mister Cartoon, a Los Angeles–based tattoo artist, sign writer, and businessman, said it best:

"NO AMOUNT . . . NO AMOUNT OF MONEY CAN COMPARE TO A JOB WELL DONE."

In the DVD *The Run Up*, a collection of interviews with twenty-six artists, he stressed, "I had to put in twenty years of work; it ain't gonna happen overnight. Success is taking out the garbage. Success is complimenting another artist."

Mister Cartoon knows that the road to happiness, and to success, is a long one, so he places his value on the quality of his work, and because of that he's been rewarded financially. He also stresses that success is far more than just a magazine cover or a coveted award—it's the component parts that equal the total sum of success. It's the things you don't see celebrated: being supportive to others in your field, maintaining a focused mind, continuing to learn. This dedication to craft rather than a quick buck is inspirational and grounding.

There are lots of different ways to achieve this mythical balance of doing what you love and getting paid for it. You could have a day job that pays the bills but spend your free time pursuing passion projects. Or you could work part-time and be disciplined so you spend two or three days a week on your side projects.

You could even develop this into freelance work that starts to pay. Spend a few years working hard and saving and then give yourself a sabbatical to fully explore your passion project and develop ways of turning it into a business.

Or find a partner and share the risk but also the passion, and turn it into a new venture. Sometimes two heads are better than one.

You could apply for work experience in an industry you want to get into. Interning at an organization is a great way to get your foot in the door and to get real-world experience. I work with two brilliant designers, Sarah Matthews and Keith Kilpin, who both joined Aardman

Digital to do work experience. They impressed us so much with their positive attitude that we never let them leave! Getting that chance to make an impression is invaluable, so don't discount the power of work experience.

There are so many ways you can work toward getting paid for doing something you love—exactly *how* will depend on your situation. There's no hard-and-fast rule, but that's a good thing. It teaches you to be fluid, flexible, and adaptive to a changing situation. And that's an invaluable skill for life!

When it all gets to be too much—and it will (working into the night can be a solitary activity!)—you just have to take a step back and remember why you're doing it. Remind yourself that you're putting happiness at the center of your plan. It's a lot easier to get that fire stoked again and get the energy levels up to help you power through tough times.

Happiness has more value than money. It's more sought after, it's rarer, and it's universal. It can't be devalued.

If you can, then never do anything for money. Do it for the love of doing it. Money comes later. Remember:

Money = Money

**Love = Satisfaction,
pride, ownership,
skills, *and* money!**

To end this chapter, here's a quote from a song by Atmosphere:

LIFE'S TOO SHORT TO BE AFRAID OF THE DARK, AND WE DON'T STOP AFTER MAKING THE MARK. SEPARATE YOUR CHEST FROM YOUR HEART, TO HELP EVERYBODY WAG YOUR TAIL WITH A LOT LESS BARK.

Atmosphere, "Let Me Know That You Know What You Want Now"

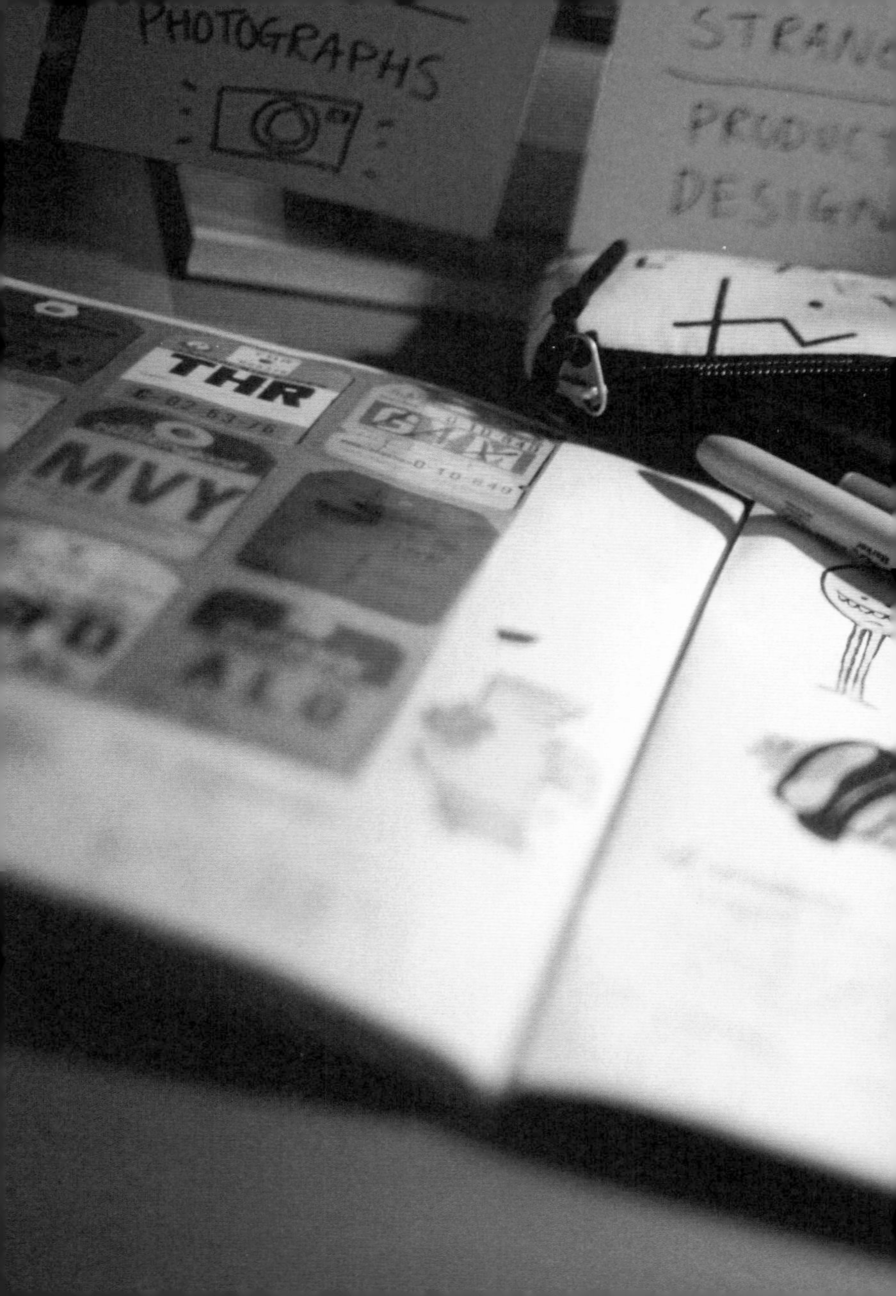
PHOTOGRAPHS
THR
MVY

3
WHAT'S
THE PLAN?

Right then! Let's get cracking! You know you want to change something, you know you want more out of life, you know you want to fly. So how do you do it? I'm glad you asked, because I have a cunning plan . . . Well, actually, it isn't that cunning. It's actually quite simple—you just have to put it into action.

A LITTLE BIT OF MY STORY

• • • • • •

It might be useful if I share a bit of my story first, to give a litte context as to why I'm saying these things. So are you sitting comfortably? Then let's begin.

I'm a thirty-three-year-old man, living in a beautiful city, with a dream job. I work as a senior designer for the digital arm of Bristol's Aardman Animations, an institution for creativity. It was founded in 1976 by two childhood friends, Peter Lord and David Sproxton. They began playing with animation on a kitchen table, using a Bolex camera that David's father, a keen amateur photographer, had at home. That experimentation gave them their first TV commission for a program called *Vision On*, which eventually led to the legendary character Morph being created. As a company, they began to grow, attracting talent like Richard Starzak and Nick Park and giving birth to some of our best-loved creations: Wallace & Gromit, Shaun the Sheep, Rex the Runt, and many more.

So, how did I come to join this prestigious place, such a cathedral of creativity? Well, as you may have guessed, not by the "normal" way. (By now, you'll have discovered there's no such thing as a "normal" path to what you love: Each route is one you have to discover yourself.)

LEFT SCHOOL

Pretty average grades—I wasn't very academic. I enjoyed art and drawing. Heard graphic design was a real job, so I thought I'd pursue that.

STUDIED AT COLLEGE

I did a Business and Technology Education Council (BTEC) National Diploma in graphic design, where I was a mediocre student who didn't yet have the "spark." I felt like I was finding my feet and learning how the world works.

DECIDED NO UNIVERSITY FOR ME

It never really had any appeal—I didn't really drink or party, and I thought that's all that university was, so I didn't apply! Instead I wanted to get into the design industry. My desire to succeed started to grow stronger.

GOT MY FIRST JOB

As a junior graphic designer in my hometown of Leicester. Learned so much: how to work with clients, how to work as part of a team.

STARTED SIDE PROJECTS

My boss encouraged me to continue my learning at home, experimenting with what I'd learned during the day job. Told me to start my own website; to upload my personal work; to share with people. That's when I started my site: jam -factory.com

GREW JAMFACTORY

As I experimented at night, I broadened my horizons and tried my hand at everything I was interested in. Skateboard design. Illustration. Photography. Filmmaking. Clothing. It was my outlet for anything and everything I enjoyed.

CONTINUED TO LEARN AT THE DAY JOB

Carried on learning at work during the day: meeting clients, taking on more responsibility, and acquiring lots of new skills.

TOOK THE PLUNGE TO GO FREELANCE

Plucked up the courage to leave my job and go it alone in the freelance world under the name of JamFactory! Helped by my friend Andy who owned a local skate shop and gave me three days' work a week, doing web design for the store. The rest of my time was my own to find new clients.

MOVED TO BRISTOL

Fell in love with the city after visiting a friend. As I never went to university, I hadn't actually lived anywhere else, so it felt like the perfect thing to do!

STARTED FROM SCRATCH

A new city meant more new clients. So I went around the city introducing myself to people and sharing my skills while continuing to add work to my website.

PUSHED MY PERSONAL PROJECTS

Now that my time was my own to manage, I balanced paid client work (usually website design) with personal projects I would upload to my website and present alongside client work. I made sure I shared my work with local networks in Bristol.

"HELLO FROM AARDMAN"

I got the most life-changing and exciting email ever, from a man named Dan Efergan. He was creative director of the digital team at Aardman Animations. He'd seen my work online and was looking for a designer to work with on a freelance project for Channel 4!

I'VE NEVER LEFT...

Eight fun-filled years later, and I'm still at Aardman. Dan is one of my closest friends, and I feel incredibly fortunate to work with such passionate and inspiring people.

SIDE PROJECTS

I'm busier than ever with my side projects. JamFactory is still going strong as my home for experimenting with new ideas and new techniques. Aardman has always supported me in what I do in my own time, which only makes me more excited to learn new things and bring them into my day job!

EXCITING FUTURE

Even as I slowly approach a decade in my dream
job, I still feel like I'm only just getting started.
Creativity is an ever-changing beast, and there's
always something new to learn and new avenues
to discover. I've had the good fortune of being
involved in different areas of Aardman, from
the digital studio to the feature-film crew.
That flexibility only inspires new challenges,
and I can't wait to see what happens next!

So that's just a snapshot of my story. What's yours?
Why not have a go at writing it down like this. It will
remind you where you've come from, where you are
now, what you've done so far—you might be surprised!
It might suggest possible next steps.

I vividly remember the young man in Leicester who felt
like he was floating and not going anywhere. It was only
in my very early twenties that I realized being creative
didn't just happen between nine and five, and that if you
put in lots of hard work, you got lots of positive vibes back.
I couldn't actually believe how simple it was. In fact, that
is what's driven me ever since: What you put in is what
you get out. So why wouldn't you want to give it your
absolute all?

JUST SAY YES

• • • • • • •

This sounds deadly obvious, doesn't it? Just say yes more, and great things will happen. Well, yep, it sorta is that easy, but it's more the state of mind you adopt that leads to new things or opens doors. Being more positive and open to new things, new places, and collaborations means you're welcoming change, and that's where new possibilities and all the fun stuff lie!

It's really easy to default to no all the time. As we grow up, we just come to expect that people are too busy or focused on their own things to say yes to others, but you'd be surprised. People do want to be helpful. They want to collaborate. You just have to ask them a question so they have the opportunity to say yes in the first place! Pull people out of their little silos and start making things together. Give them opportunities, and they'll give you opportunities!

You'll be totally surprised where it can take you once you say yes to an opportunity. It may connect you with other like-minded people, show you new things, and, most importantly, set a precedent so you continue to move forward with this positive and open mindset.

There's a flipside to this though (sorry!), which we come to in the next section . . .

LUCK IS WHAT HAPPENS WHEN PREPARATION MEETS OPPORTUNITY.

Seneca

"OPPORTUNITY DOES NOT KNOCK; IT PRESENTS ITSELF WHEN YOU BEAT DOWN THE DOOR."

Kyle Chandler

DON'T WAIT TO BE ASKED

• • • • • •

The previous point of "Just say yes" makes it sound as if there's a life-changing opportunity just waiting for you around every corner. I'm sorry to be the bearer of bad news, but that's simply not true. You do have to make yourself open and ready for opportunities, should they appear (which is about saying yes), but more importantly it's about not waiting for those chances to come to you. You should try and bring them to yourself.

Ol' Kyle hits the nail on the head up there. Not part of an arts collective? Start your own. Want to see a film on the decline of the cotton candy industry? Make the movie. Want a skateboard graphic featuring kittens? Create a board company yourself.

Many projects I've been involved in, I actually started myself because the opportunity wasn't there to begin with. I've made countless T-shirts just because I wanted to wear a particular design and couldn't find it. (Tip: If you do this, make a few extra, too, y'know, for your mom and your brother to wear.)

Then the next time you do it, you'll discover a few more people want to get involved, and things just grow and grow. When you dedicate your time to making something you honestly believe in, people want you to do well.

Every business, every venture, every endeavor started from nothing. They all started with just an idea. But the idea alone isn't enough. Someone has to make it happen. Someone has to commit to it. So make sure you commit!

This very book you're reading happened because I emailed Miranda, founder of Do Books, introducing myself and saying that I would love to write a book. A year and some exciting meetings later, here we are!

Similarly, Miranda told me that the book company itself happened after she watched a Do Lecture online, then emailed the info@ address asking if they'd ever considered publishing books by their speakers. So the book that you are holding and the publishing house that produced it were just an idea once, too. How cool is that?

This doesn't mean that every opportunity is ripe for the picking. For every positive outcome, nine of them will have ended in rejection. That's fine though—you need those negative outcomes to fuel your journey onward. Sure, you have to stop and have a little cry and a good tantrum, but those feelings of frustration are fleeting. Go and have a skate, a run, or a bike ride. Things might look different after that.

Every month, I have setbacks and nonstarters. If I see something I'm into, I often email or message the people involved, share my excitement and desire to collaborate, and more often than not I never hear back. Not a peep. But that's okay. In the words of Thomas Edison, "I have not failed. I've just found 10,000 ways that won't work."

You don't have to be an inventor to apply that to your life and the pursuit of your goals.

"AUTODIDACTICISM," OR THE ART OF TEACHING YOURSELF

• • • • • •

Autodidacticism. It sounds super-smart and dropping it casually into conversations makes you sound like a brainbox, but really it's not all that fancy. It simply means "self-learning." More accurately, it's learning about subjects with little or no formal education. With Wikipedia at our fingertips and YouTube tutorials just a tap away, there has never been a better time to teach yourself a new skill or find a new passion.

And there's nothing more satisfying. You might pick up a tiny little nugget of information that lets you totally own the next pub quiz, or it could be a whole new field that changes your entire life. It's quite easy to think, and feel, that you're already on a set course. That you learn certain things early on in life and then spend the rest of your time honing in on that one thing. But it doesn't have to be that way. You might find yourself watching a documentary on the history of salsa dancing, when you suddenly realize you have a secret burning desire to become a salsa teacher.

Or you discover you've actually got a real good rap flow and a lifetime as a grime MC awaits you.

You've seen it a hundred times, too. The outsider who comes to a new town or into a new job in an unorthodox way and, despite the odds being stacked against them, works hard to prove their worth and eventually wins the respect of their peers. Oh, and gets the girl.

Fade to black. Credits roll.

See, it's a recurring motif of Hollywood films. Everyone loves an underdog story. Even the simple act of trying to take on a new discipline outside of the "proper" framework or path is often seen as a pretty crazy thing to do (especially by your friends), but it doesn't have to be.

The point is, don't deny these urges to learn and discover. The more you open yourself up to new things, the more you'll crave. They don't all have to be new careers, they can be new hobbies or even new friendships. The things you do define who you are, and bringing those new interests into your work can take you in new directions, spark a conversation with someone new, and lead to a new side project, a new role, or a promotion.

That doesn't mean to say it's easy and that with all this expert-led information at our fingertips everyone can become skilled in anything they choose without much thought. These are just tools that allow us to access the information more quickly. We still have to bring our own curiosity, patience, and drive. If anything, we have to work harder to filter out that external noise, the myriad "things" vying for our attention. Just as we have a mass of tools that allow us to do anything, we need to find other tools and methods to help us stay focused and keep us on track!

Just writing this book right now, I've got my preferred text editor in full-screen with no other interface, and I've got my noise-cancelling headphones on while a website plays random mellow sounds of fire crackling and rain falling. You've got to exercise a bit of self-discipline, especially when you're being the student, researcher, and, to some degree, teacher too.

All that said, we need a little bit of that guidance and even fear now and again to help keep us moving forward. As much as we do not miss that teacher who would yell at us if we weren't paying attention, they did get us to focus on the task in hand! (Note to self: Develop app featuring unstable teachers screaming terrifying words of encouragement/disdain at random intervals.)

Don't be too hard on yourself if you're finding it difficult to stay focused. It's a tricky thing to keep your mind zoned into learning something new, especially when real life is happening around you, eager to pull you back to reality without hesitation. So first of all, shake off any frustrations that you aren't learning as quickly—or staying as motivated—as you'd like. It's tough, it takes time, and everyone finds it hard. Don't let those niggles of self-doubt stop you before you can even begin—just start moving and you'll build momentum before you know it!

The other thing is to set yourself small achievable goals and then reward yourself. Write three paragraphs before bed. Read an article before breakfast. Memorize one inspiring quote per week. It can be anything—progress is progress. Reward yourself with that cake I saw you eyeing in the market, or let yourself watch that TV show you've been looking forward to. Pretty soon you'll be setting bigger goals and pushing yourself to learn more. Exercising your own discipline will be your own motivation.

Self-learning doesn't ever have to stop. Most of us finish education very early on in life, but we never ever stop being a student . . . and the best part of it? We can teach ourselves anything we like.

TINKERING IS WHAT HAPPENS WHEN YOU TRY SOMETHING YOU DON'T QUITE KNOW HOW TO DO, GUIDED BY WHIM, IMAGINATION, AND CURIOSITY.

Exploratorium museum, San Francisco

ONE-NIGHTERS AND
SELF-IMPOSED DEADLINES

• • • • • •

Sometimes getting started is just as difficult as finishing something. You have every reason in the world to put it off:

— I don't have time to dedicate to it.

— It's not the right time.

— I don't have the money needed right now.

— I'm tired.

— *Game of Thrones* is on TV.

There are always plenty of reasons for not starting a new project or venture, and some of them are valid, and some of them aren't. But the thing is, it is hard starting something new. It does take a lot of energy and willpower, which is precious and hard to come by. That's why I like to do little bite-size chunks of "new."

I call them "one-nighters"; I indulge myself in a new microproject but give myself only one evening. The end result is normally a silly little video or a poster for a fictional band, but I get something out of it! Now, I'm talking in design terms, as that's what I do, but it doesn't have to be at all. You could write a short story. Compose a fifteen-second opera. Organize a coffee morning. Try out a new recipe. Whatever it is, you get something out of it.

Think of it as training. In order to get fit, you have to exercise. Small bursts of exertion to build up the muscle mass to get fitter and stronger. You can't run a marathon without doing a few 10ks first, so get those little-and-often training exercises under your belt, and you'll soon find yourself flying past your competitors.

PERSONAL PROJECTS
ARE PERSONAL

• • • • • •

As you can probably tell by now, I'm a huge advocate of personal projects. I think they're a great way to learn new skills and delve into areas that are new to you. The difference with personal projects is that they're exactly that—*personal*. You can pour your heart and soul into them. They're honest and authentic.

It's always good to work on that big project for that important client, winning that prestigious award (if we're lucky!), but rarely are these a truly unique endeavor by one person. That's what makes personal projects different and special. You can totally indulge yourself—your own ideas, curiosities, for better or for worse. It'll make you a more-rounded person and, as a creative, you can continually push your own boundaries. Not only that, but you will better understand how you work and your own workflow, which you can then apply to your non-personal projects.

The beauty is that these projects can be whatever you want them to be, with no agenda at all, other than your own satisfaction. I really recommend to just do it, no matter how silly, even if it's something that only you understand—get it out of your brain and into the real world.

"IN THE PARTICULAR IS CONTAINED THE UNIVERSAL."

James Joyce

I first heard this quote in a talk from the wonderfully inspiring James Victore. James is also a former Do Lectures speaker and the artist behind all the Do Book covers. I had to read it through a few times to process it. By making something so personal, so honest, so *you*, it becomes universal. It becomes universal because it's human. It has those perfect flaws that we know can only come from a real individual making something that means everything to them. And don't forget, you don't have to share anything unless you want to. Use this time to experiment and play. Find your voice. Find what excites you.

So, what are you gonna make?

QUALITY OR QUANTITY?

• • • • • •

I don't think you have to choose—you can have both. I believe that quantity can make quality! Malcolm Gladwell wrote that it takes ten thousand hours of practice to achieve mastery of a particular task, which is another way of saying, "Practice makes perfect." And that's something your mother told you constantly anyway.

So how does this seemingly obvious piece of information help us? For one thing, it gives us perspective. It's so easy now—especially because we have the necessary tools at our disposal—to expect to be good at something really quickly. I can find a how-to on YouTube within seconds, order an instruction book from Amazon and have it delivered the same day. The rapidness of getting the information doesn't really correlate with the pace of the actual learning. This makes us frustrated.

That's when you have to take a step back and remember it's all about doing. Learn by doing. The theory's all fine and gravy, but you just have to get stuck in and do the time. Put in the hours.

My boss once told me, "You're only as good as your last piece of work." She totally nailed it there. You should give every piece of work, every undertaking, your full undivided energy, effort, and enthusiasm. It should be the best thing you've ever created or contributed to. Then you do something new and start that process all over again, once again, giving it your all.

Every time you repeat that cycle, you'll bring new nuggets of learning with you, micro-adjustments of knowing what works and doesn't work in a particular situation. You'll be able to subconsciously identify patterns and problems and steer yourself toward or away from them.

You are learning the shorthand of your own brain, and that's a powerful thing. But there are no shortcuts. Grime artist Jme said it best:

"GOTTA PUT IN THAT WORK."

BE KIND

• • • • • •

Comedian, TV host, and ex-*Simpsons* writer Conan O'Brien summed things up perfectly in the farewell speech from his long-running TV career:

> **"NOBODY IN LIFE GETS EXACTLY WHAT THEY THOUGHT THEY WERE GOING TO GET, BUT IF YOU WORK REALLY HARD, AND YOU'RE KIND, AMAZING THINGS WILL HAPPEN."**

I've always loved this quote. It's totally honest. Hard work is just one piece of the puzzle—being kind and being positive are the other parts. It's really easy to become negative. We're surrounded by the stuff, especially in the media. You have to work twice as hard to stay positive, but here's the thing—once you've brought that positivity to the surface, it becomes a catalyst in itself. It's a really infectious feeling! Problems become challenges to overcome, not insurmountable hurdles.

Things get tough. That's just a fact of life. But if you can approach challenges with a positive mental attitude, you'll find you can handle things a lot better. You spend your time fighting to get through it, rather than treading water wondering, "Why me?" (That's not to say you can't have a good old wallow now and then. But you'll feel a lot better once you start swimming!)

It's also infectious and gives a welcome boost to other people, especially if you're collaborating and creating things together. It's really easy to say no when working on ideas with others. Try saying "Yes, and . . ." and see how that feels instead. It pushes things forward and keeps ideas evolving rather than getting stuck in a never-ending loop of wounded pride.

In the end, it's all about a state of mind. Going forward instead of back, being open to change and challenge, knowing you can overcome it. All of it. Any of it. Think positive. Be positive. And be kind and respectful to each other.

FIND A MENTOR;
BE A MENTOR

• • • • • •

For the most part, your journey is traveled alone. It is as unique as you are and will take unexpected twists and turns—all part of the fun, of course!

That doesn't mean to say you shouldn't have companions along the way though, and a mentor is an absolutely invaluable guide. Any journey toward "being your best self" is a long and sometimes confusing one, so to have someone you can call on, who is perhaps a few steps ahead of you and is willing to share some of their own wisdom and experiences . . . well, that's pure magic.

So how do you get a mentor? Kidnap is always an option but makes it a bit hard to establish any rapport, so maybe not. The other much nicer and more ethical way is simply to ask. A mentor isn't some ethereal Obi-Wan spirit that's always around you. It can be someone you email once a year. It can be someone you call once a fortnight. There are no hard-and-fast rules for how to be a mentor or how to be mentored.

I'm lucky enough to have a few mentors whom I admire greatly—yes, you can have more than one! I'm forever asking them questions and learning from their knowledge. They are all extremely patient with me, and I couldn't be more appreciative. My friend Merlin Crossingham shares with me his knowledge of filmmaking and animation. Dan Efergan has been my mentor ever since I joined Aardman, and he freely shares with me how he creatively directs himself, his projects, and his team of colleagues. You learn so much from doing, but you also learn so much from just listening.

If you can find people who inspire you, people who are doing what you want to do, talk to them. Find out their names. Give them a call. Drop them an email. Make contact. Tell them who you are, what you're doing, and whether they mind if you ask them some questions; maybe suggest a cuppa. Then if you want, just ask them outright if they'd mind mentoring you. It's a flattering thing to be asked, so don't be afraid.

There's no limit on how many mentors you can have. You'll find that different people—depending on their location, their available time, their connection to you— will bring something different to your relationship. Have a couple; have five. It's up to you!

It's not a one-way street either. Make sure you return the favor and become a mentor for others. As you learn and progress, whatever stage you're at in your career, your experiences can really help others, so make yourself open to becoming a mentor. It'll probably be the most rewarding thing you ever do.

THE GREATEST MISTAKE YOU CAN MAKE IN LIFE IS TO BE CONTINUALLY FEARING YOU WILL MAKE ONE.

Elbert Hubbard

NETWORKING—HOW ABOUT "NICECHATFUNTIME" PARTY?

• • • • • •

Networking. The word alone strikes fear into the hearts of many. It sounds so impersonal, so forced, as if you have an agenda from the outset. But the thing is, you know that everyone just wants the same thing: to meet like-minded people, who have shared interests and passions, which may even lead to a productive and fruitful working relationship! Unfortunately, all that goes out the window the minute you think of it as "networking"!

I'm asking you to cast aside that negative term, and in your mind to rebrand it as "NiceChatFunTime." Once you do that, you'll find yourself signing up for all sorts of meet-ups and get-togethers. Getting together with other people in your field (and outside of it, too) is always beneficial. There's never a downside to meeting new people. You might come away with the biggest contract of your life—or your new best friend.

Even better than attending these things is creating your own. If you're thinking that there's never anything for you where you live, nothing that whets your appetite, then I guarantee you that others will be feeling the same. Why not put on an event? Find a location, pick a theme, get some chips—that's pretty much all you need to get people together. To be honest, you don't even need a location or a theme, just a bag of chips and a table at your local pub is enough. Just throw in a dash of enthusiasm and some ice-breakers to get people talking.

Don't wait for someone else to create the thing you want to see, the type of event you want to go to. Jump in and make it happen yourself. Build it, and they will come. Just have chips.

4

HOW CAN I
STAND OUT?

The thing about making your mark on the world and pursuing exciting things is that you're not the only one doing it. But that's encouraging, right? That means there might be a support network out there, other people that you can relate to. On the flip side, you risk finding yourself smack-bang in the middle of a very crowded market.

So how do you stand out? Well, you can start by being true. You should never resort to *Apprentice*-style backstabbing sociopathic tendencies to get ahead. Why? Because a) it's really mean, and b) it's totally unnecessary! This section looks at a few ways you can shine by being an honest, engaged, and positive person.

Rest assured, good people and good work always rise to the top. It might take a while though, so stay positive. For now, here are a few pointers.

DON'T WORRY ABOUT BEING ORIGINAL; BE HONEST

• • • • • •

I know this is a bold statement, but stick with me. First, if you do have the power to be a true original, a true visionary, then well done. You can skip this part!

If, like me, you're among the 99.9 percent who aren't world-leading visionaries right out of the gate, then this part is for you. Much like worrying about what other people's lives are like, you can't spend your energy or time worrying about doing something no one has done before. Because, dude, that's really, really, *really* hard.

Instead, concentrate on making and doing things you believe in. Do things that you love and can pour your heart into. Build on what others have built, but do it honestly. You never know, you might just stumble across something totally original.

As an individual, you are unique. Yes, you'll have lots of things in common with your friends and peers, but you would still create something totally different than a friend who had the exact same interests as you. Your upbringing, your outlook, your loves, your hates, your passions, your fears—all that gets melted down into a sticky goo of creative lava, and what solidifies out of that primordial ooze is totally unique to you. It may have similarities in look or tone, but dig a little deeper and you'll find that the underlying reasons for its particular form are totally personal.

That's why there's no point getting hung up on comparison. It's something you can't ever avoid, so just expect it will happen and carry on past it. It can be crippling when someone says, "Oh yeah, I've seen that, it's just like X"—even though you've never heard of X or you know you've taken a totally different route to get there. Don't let that stop you, put it in the back of your mind and carry on regardless.

A Bristol friend named Miles once told me, "Don't make it perfect; make it now." I've never forgotten that.

BEING A POLYMATH

• • • • • •

I love the term *polymath*. We don't hear it so much these days, yet I always think it sounds really romantic and quite old world. A polymath is a person whose expertise spans a significant number of different subject areas— and I'd really like to see the term come back into our everyday language.

As businesses and careers have grown more specific and focused, they have required people to fit into particular roles and tick very specific boxes. That's absolutely fine, and it makes sense from an efficiency point of view but not from a human-being point of view.

Our tastes and interests vary all the time—that's what makes us unique and interesting. We smash all of our influences and passions together to make us *us*. I'm not saying you have to find a new job that perfectly blends your passion for brain surgery with your love of interior decorating—that would be difficult and quite weird. I am saying it's up to us to push that mindset forward. To accept that individuals aren't just focused on the task at hand.

We should be encouraged to draw from all the other stuff that makes us tick, to help solve problems and make things better.

Here are some inspirational folk who will guide you on your way to polymathdom:

— **Leonardo da Vinci** *(1452–1519)* is probably one of the most famous polymaths of all time. He was a painter, sculptor, architect, musician, mathematician, engineer, inventor . . . the list goes on.

— **Hildegard of Bingen** *(1098–1179)* was a writer, composer, philosopher, and mystic, all while keeping up her godly duties of running an abbey.

— **Takeshi Kitano** *(1947–)* is a film director, comedian, singer, presenter, painter, and video game designer. He sees entertainment as his focus but applies his talents in all sorts of different ways.

— **Noam Chomsky** *(1928–)* is an American linguist, philosopher, cognitive scientist, logician, political commentator, social justice activist, and anarcho-syndicalist advocate.

That's not a bad list, is it? Of course, it's useful to have a key strength that you can be known for and to use as a bedrock for your own career path. Take the experiences you have gained through work and other environments and build on them. But don't shy away from continuing to develop other pursuits. You'll be amazed at the number of times you apply knowledge gained from other "fields" to a particular task. You will have a broader skill set to deploy, and a wider frame of reference to draw on.

You can achieve the fabled status of polymath in a lot of different ways. The first one is to read, read, and read some more. Fill your brain with new knowledge, go as deep down the rabbit hole as you can. If you fancy something totally radical, then why not pack your bags and travel? Visit the places connected with your new branch of learning, maybe even do some work experience in your new location; immerse yourself in a new culture.

Don't worry though; not every path to becoming a polymath has to be so extreme. It's up to you how far you go, but it should scare you, even if just a little. Give the heart a flutter. It will be a springboard to new and exciting things.

To be multidisciplinary is super useful. Employers really value it—it's a sign of being proactive. Sure, you can (and should) have your core strength that you're hired for (e.g., a sign writer or a dancer), but when you can wow people by showing them that you can also make a film about it, design a logo, and organize an event based around it all . . . that's impressive.

Pretty soon people stop thinking of you for one thing, and just trust you to do it all. And that's when you're well on your way to becoming a polymath! A lot of value is place on skilled people. Make yourself invaluable.

Albert Camus was an existentialist philosopher, playwright, member of the French Resistance, and international goalkeeper for Algeria. Now the next time a career advisor tells you that you can't be a soccer player and a philosopher, you tell them about Albert. It's like career alchemy!

BE THE SUN, NOT THE WIND.

BE THE SUN, NOT THE WIND

• • • • • • •

I was having a discussion with my friend Laura at work about positivity, and she said, "Be the sun, not the wind." She was referring to Aesop's fable "The North Wind and the Sun," which goes a little bit like this:

The North Wind and the Sun decide to have a little competition to see who's stronger. They see a fella walking along a path and agree to see who can make him remove his cloak first. The Wind—who's a bit of a jerk, to be honest—says he'll go first and proceeds to brashly blow a gale, using all his might to force the cloak from the man's shoulders. But all that happens is the poor guy clutches at his cloak even tighter, pulling it around his body.

The Wind decides he's had enough and lets the Sun give it a shot. The big yellow blighter calmly rises, shuts his eyes, and glows as bright as he can. Lo and behold, the man quickly takes off his cloak, lays it on the floor, and sits down to enjoy the rays of sunshine.

The moral of the story? Always be nice, and people will take off their clothes for you.

Just kidding. I mean, always be nice and positive, use your skills for good, and you'll be surprised what can happen.

BE FLUID AND FLEXIBLE

• • • • • •

Everything changes. From the weather to world politics, things are always in a state of flux. We expect things like technology to change, but less so our attitudes about *how* we do things. Why is that? Shouldn't they be just as upgradable as your smartphone?

You will have new situations thrown at you all the time, so you'll need to be prepared and have a few tools to deal with them. Those tools aren't necessarily physical objects— they can be new practices.

Opening yourself to change, allowing yourself and your thought processes to be questioned, is a huge and liberating affair. It's difficult, of course, as you spend your life learning by your experiences and the mistakes you've made—but don't be afraid to stop, look back, and pull apart what you know.

It's a tricky and emotional process, but it's one I think is vital. It's a practice I'm only just learning myself, as I get older and go through new experiences. When I was younger I'd make a decision, stick with it, and assume it had been dealt with. Fair enough; I was making the decision based on the information I had at the time. But if I had to make the same decision today, not only might I make a different decision, but hopefully I'd be more open to changing it as my experience grew.

This has all become a bit heavy now, hasn't it? Sorry. Let's just chill for a minute . . .

So, what I mean is, try to allow yourself to be fluid and flexible in everything you do. It will make you more of a balanced individual and allow you to take that important step back and evaluate things, without fearing change.

Client changes the brief?
Sure, no problem. Things change.

Scrap the second half of your novel?
Okey-dokey, things change.

Painted that thing the wrong color?
Cool. Sand it down and start afresh.

Being fluid is a powerful thing. You can flow when you want to, become solid when you need to, and transform into something new whenever you choose to.

5

SETBACKS AND HOW TO DEAL WITH THEM

This is where it gets really tricky when you're facing adversity. How do you deal with your own worst enemy? What happens when you just can't see the forest for the trees? What do you do when THE FLIPPING PRINTER JUST WON'T PRINT THE FLIPPING PAGE?

Phew . . . sorry. I always get a bit frustrated when things go wrong. That's fine though; that's natural—you can't really stop being overwhelmed. It's an emotion you don't have much control over. What you do have control over though, is what you do after you've identified that it's happening.

The easiest route is to simply give up, drop it, and run. Please don't. Stick with it—you'll feel so much better for working through it. So when you get thrown a curveball, here are a few tips on how to smash it out of the park.

YOU'RE A GHOST DRIVING A MEAT-COVERED SKELETON MADE FROM STARDUST.

Source unknown

GET PERSPECTIVE

• • • • • •

It's really easy to zone in on a particular project and let the pressure pile up, warping your sense of scale. I like to take a step back (it doesn't have to be a big step). You'll find that as soon as you switch to a wider view, it's easier to remember that we really are just meat bags made from carbon, and that the client problem you've been killing yourself over doesn't matter as much as you thought.

Now that's not to say it doesn't matter at all. It just frees you up to pop that particular problem in a different part of your brain—the "Hey, this is a problem that needs solving, I'm good at that, let's solve it" part, rather than the "AGGHHH!?!!?! PANIC! OVERREACT! SCREAM!!" part. This whole section could otherwise just read, "Take a step back and breathe."

Right now, in the age of perpetual media overload, it's really easy to get a warped perspective on what matters and specifically what matters to you, which in turn really affects what you spend your energy caring about. And that energy is a really precious thing!

It's all about concern versus control. If you indulge the news channels and the big media outlets then they'd have you believe that things like the lives of celebrities, the latest natural disaster, and the war in a far-off land are all things you should be concerned about. I disagree. That sounds quite cold; right? But I think concern and care are two different things. You should care about those things, if you want to, of course, but you can't let them concern you, because you have no control over them.

That's where the "circle of control" (see the diagram on the next page) comes into play, examining the things you can change and can spend your finite energy on. Your attitude and enthusiasm, your legacy in life, the skills you learn and more—these are the things you can change. These are the things that can make you happier and your life richer.

Your energy is a very important resource, and sometimes you have to really dig to uncover it, so treat it with respect and invest this valuable commodity only in what matters most to you (with the occasional splurge on something totally indulgent, just for fun).

CIRCLE OF
CONCERN

Time and energy wasted on reacting to
issues you cannot control

**WHAT CAN
CONCERN YOU**

**Political views
of others**

**What others
think of you**

**Natural
disasters**

**Personal lives
of celebrities and politicians**

**The
news**

**The
economy**

**The
weather**

**Weapons, war,
terrorist threats**

BEING
REACTIVE

CIRCLE OF
CONTROL

Time and energy spent focusing on
issues you *can* control

Where you work

**Businesses
you start**

**Places
you visit**

**What
you read**

**Your attitude
and enthusiasm**

**What
you buy**

**Where
you live**

**What skills
you learn**

**Leadership positions
you hold**

*WHAT YOU
CAN CONTROL*

BEING
PROACTIVE

THE REASON WE STRUGGLE WITH INSECURITY IS THAT WE COMPARE OUR BEHIND-THE-SCENES WITH EVERYONE ELSE'S HIGHLIGHTS REEL.

Steve Furtick

STOP BEING SO INSECURE!

• • • • • •

This quote is spot on, especially for the age of Instagram, where you only have to do a quick scroll to see someone you admire doing things you can only dream of, at a level that seems totally unobtainable! Yes, of course those people you look up to work hard, put in the hours, and dedicate their life to their craft, but don't forget that feed is edited and curated—it's their highlights reel!

You don't see the tweet at 1:06 a.m. where ol' Bobby Big Deal is worrying about securing his next piece of work, wondering if he really has what it takes to deliver. Or you don't get the Instagram post where Suzie Slick feels lost, unhappy, and unsure of what to do next.

The point is, they're human beings like you and me. They worry, stress, cry, shout, and fuss like everyone else. They doubt themselves, hate themselves, and then come through the other side, just like you and me.

Let your heroes inspire you but let them encourage you further by knowing they have the exact same worries and problems that you do. In the meantime, take inspiration from your Instagram feed. And if it doesn't inspire you, start following people who do.

TIME

• • • • • •

Time's a slippery snake: When you need more, it goes faster, and when you want to speed things up a notch, it seems to slow right down. I would love to let you in on the secret to controlling time, but we all know it doesn't exist.

The reality, however, is exciting and liberating. You have the same twenty-four hours as everyone else. On the surface, that sounds depressing; right? "Okay, we all have the same number of hours in a day to try to get everything done." Well, yeah, you could think of it that way. Another way I like to think of it is:

I have the same amount of time in which to create as Mozart did!

Or:

Marie Curie and I are time buddies!

The point is, everyone else in history—our heroes, the people we look up to and admire—have had the same time constraints as we do. And at some point, they will have said, "Oh, I say, there's just not enough hours in the day!"

No one has the time—you have to make the time. These people have gone on to make things, do things, create things that changed the world. Yes, yes, yes, I know that's because they're immensely talented, but creation isn't just about talent—that's only half of it. You've got to do the work. You can be the smartest cat in the room, but if you choose to sit on the sofa eating Cheetos all day, nothing's gonna get done!

Here's the other thing. It's not about working more hours; it's about being smarter with your time. We have to be clever about what we spend our time on. For me, it's about spreading it between all my passions: family, friends, work, play, personal projects, well-being. That's why it's tricky. If it was purely about putting in the hours, then that'd be easy: I'd tell you to work for twenty-three hours a day and sleep for one. But that's bonkers and definitely not the answer. It's a delicate balancing act that's personal to you and your situation. You have to decide when, where, and how you'll spend those precious ticks and tocks.

"TIME IS THE MOST VALUABLE THING A MAN CAN SPEND."

Theophrastus

FINDING THE BALANCE

• • • • • •

Much like finding the time, I'm afraid that finding the balance is really difficult! That's because it's different for everyone. It's like alchemy: a magical and mystical combination of ingredients to achieve the perfect recipe for a harmonious life. It will pay to find more balance, because you'll find yourself more productive, healthier, and happier if you can find the groove that works for you.

What's more, your balance will be ever shifting. You need to constantly review what you're doing and how you're feeling to see what's working for you. The good news is, it gets easier the more you do it. You'll notice patterns of when you're grumpy and tired (because you start asking yourself, "Why am I grumpy and tired?") and once you start to identify your own patterns, you can rectify them much more easily and quickly.

"Why are you rambling on about balance though?" I can hear you scream, albeit quietly and calmly. Well, because I don't think the attitude "Work more hours than anyone else" is right, nor is it enough to really succeed and be happy. What you achieve in eighteen hours might have only the same value as someone who's beavered away for three hours. It isn't about volume; it's about substance, and you can give your best to something only when your body and brain are satisfied.

Seeing your friends, having a quiet night in, watching something new, playing a game, making a nice meal for your family, going to a new place, revisiting an old place, learning a language, walking the dog, running a race, listening to music, laughing your head off at something silly. You need to be a human being to experience the world around you with people beside you. It'll make you a better "DOer," I promise!

On the next page is a little snapshot of my work/life balance at the moment, what's working for me right now (as a thirty-three-year-old full-time employed married man with a dog—it might be very different if you're forty-two and have a couple of kids, or if you're a seventy-two-year-old retiree).

WEEKDAYS

• • •

Get up an hour early before work to write this book.
An early start works better for me to write.

•

Get ready and walk the dog, which wakes me up properly.

•

Work 9:30 a.m. to 6 p.m. at my day job, which I love—
grab some lunch with my colleagues, and then spend the
rest of lunch catching up with another colleague
on a personal project we're working on.

•

Finish work, cycle home, and spend time with my wife
and dog, catching up on the day. Have a quick play on the
drums or PS4 before cooking dinner to unwind a little.

•

Eat together with my wife, Jane, watch a
little thirty-minute episode of a TV show.

•

Get productive again around 9 p.m., where Jane and I get
stuck into personal projects.

•

Work straight until about midnight, sometimes later,
sometimes earlier, then it's time for bed!

WEEKENDS

• • •

I treat the working week as the time I try to be
as productive as possible, so that on weekends
I can relax a lot more.

I treat the working week as the time I try to be
as productive as possible, so that on weekends
I can relax a lot more.

Both Jane and I work on weekends a bit, depending
on what's going on, but if we do put in a few hours,
we make sure we relax in the evenings and get a good
night's rest. That way, we're ready for a new week!

This is just what's working for me now, and I didn't always
work like this—I used to work absolutely every hour, took
on way too much, was ill quite a lot, and never saw anyone!
Now I'm much better and, with a supportive, encouraging,
and understanding wife, I feel much more peaceful and
productive.

Working hard isn't just about hard work, it's about
being self-disciplined, to stay refreshed and energized so
that when you are working hard, it's pure gold (hopefully).

KEEP YOUR HOPES UP HIGH AND YOUR HEAD DOWN LOW.

A Day to Remember, "All I Want"

DEALING WITH STRESS

· · · · · ·

Stuff gets stressful. Choosing a vocation gets stressful. Looking for work gets stressful. Work itself gets stressful. Deadlines are stressful. (They're called DEADlines—it's a bit intense, isn't it?)

Me simply telling you to avoid stress really doesn't help much. Whatever your position, whether you're in education or employment, full-time or freelance, it can all get a bit too much sometimes. So, I've racked my brains to think of some positives around stress, and I finally found something!

For starters, stressing around something can mean that you care a great deal about it and that you want to do a good job. When you feel that stress creep around your shoulders, don't let it curdle your enthusiasm for your end goal. That daunting feeling might just be the crescendo before the big finale! Once you're through it, that sense of completion and satisfaction is amplified.

This leads me to the other part of it: There's always an end point. Hindsight's a wonderful thing because you tend to look back and think, "Well, that wasn't so bad."

When it all gets to be bit too much, try and remember how sweet that end point is and that you will always, no matter how difficult it seems, get there in the end.

Try to be patient, too. Sometimes frustration can come when you're working with a particular system or with other people. Remember, they're doing their job and may do it differently, but that's because they're not you! Be kind and communicate—you're all in this together. Memories are forged in the madness.

Lastly, remember it's just a thing. It's not life or death (unless you're working in an emergency room). Recently I watched an incredible BBC documentary that really helped me put stress in perspective. The Amazonian Sateré-Mawé tribe has an initiation ritual for the pre-adolescent boys of the clan. They must wear a pair of gloves that has hundreds of sedated bullet ants (named because their sting is said to feel like getting shot) sewn into it. Once the boys have the gloves on their hands, the ants are woken up and they proceed to sting. Continuously. The boys must stand and take the pain for ten minutes until the elders allow them to remove their hands from the gloves. This rite of passage happens as many times as needed, until the boy is said to be a real warrior.

So the next time that deadline fills you with dread, or the revision gives you nightmares, or you're simply not where you want to be, remember that you've got to work through it—it's just a temporary state of toughness that will lead to a positive outcome, and not an unbelievably painful agony-filled series of trials involving angry insects. *That's* stressful.

FINISH THINGS

• • • • • •

We all know the feeling: you're halfway through a project, and the love has totally gone. Evaporated. Poof! Or you're stuck at the first hurdle, waiting for the lightning bolt of an idea to hit you, but nothing's happening. Even the magnitude of a big decision can be so all-consuming that you simply can't work out what to do next. It's so tempting to abandon it, put on the TV, and forget about the whole thing, but I'm here to encourage you to see it through to the end.

You've done the groundwork, you've put in the energy and effort to get your idea off the ground—which is the hardest part—or maybe you're helping out someone and, for whatever reason, it's turned into a nightmare. There are so many scenarios where a seemingly enjoyable thing turns into something that's no fun at all.

Maybe you're yet to have that big idea. You're going round in circles in your mind, trying to conjure up something that will stick, but nothing feels right and you feel as if you're fighting a losing battle with yourself.

Perhaps you're at that first crossroads, unsure of what to do next—college or university, further education or employment, climbing the corporate ladder or quitting and going out on your own? These decisions can get so overwhelming that they become paralyzing. You will always be your own worst enemy—you've got to know when to silence that critic and just persevere, despite your frustrations.

You basically have two options: the easy way or the hard way. The easy way is packing it in and erasing it from your memory, sticking to the status quo. The hard way is battling through the frustrations and finishing something, or even just making a firm decision. The good news is that that route comes packed with its own sweet reward—satisfaction! It's really hard to remember that feeling when you're in the thick of it, but just remember to always be moving forward, no matter what the pace. You'll have taken a big step just because you didn't quit. And soon you'll hit your stride!

The same can be true if you're working with other people on something. Standing by them, giving it your all, and seeing it through to the bitter end with them is an admirable thing. Mind you: be sure to communicate your frustrations and doubts when you can to help everyone avoid another painful situation.

However tricky the process was at the time, once it's complete you'll be able to look back and analyze what made it so complicated and what you can take away from that, good or bad. Neither new knowledge nor new perspective is ever a bad thing, however you came by it, and having it means you can move on to something new and exciting.

Think of it as a boss level in a video game. It might beat you down and you might lose a life or two. Heck, you might even have a fit and throw your controller on the floor along the way—but in the end the win will feel all the more sweet.

APATHY IS THE ENEMY

• • • • • •

There seems to be a notion that being passionate about something isn't cool. I'm not sure where this comes from, but, especially in school, actively pursuing a hobby or a subject that excited you seemed to make you a nerd. When I was a kid, you were a "boff" if you excelled in something or showed a keen interest in learning. Now I can't get into the psychology of it because I have absolutely no clue why it happens, but I do know that it can be damaging. Being a teenager is confusing enough, so doing anything that might put you at odds with your peers is terrifying—and consequently most of us avoid it like the plague.

The sooner we snap out of that mentality, the better. We need different, weird, strange people to dream up different, weird, and strange solutions to our problems. As adults, we need to help break down the stigma attached to anything outside of the "norm." The word geek is a prime example. Ten years ago, if you were a geek then you were deemed to have a certain look, a closed set of interests, and little of value to offer the world. Now the likes of Elon Musk and Anita Sengupta are celebrated for their incredible achievements and pioneering work.

We need to make heroes of those who DO. We should put the people who create and contribute to our world on pedestals and celebrate them the world over. Media sensationalism and reality television have given us a warped sense of importance, of valuing doing nothing over doing something. It's hard work, but we have to constantly reassess what's important to us, what matters, and who we want to spend our time listening to.

I don't need to stress this though, because you're reading a DO book. You're already engaged and active. We just need to amplify that feeling of apathy being the enemy and know that we can all create and contribute to our world, however cool (or not) we think we are.

> ## "YOU MUST PARTICIPATE IN THE CREATIVE WORLD YOU WANT TO BECOME PART OF. SO WHAT IF YOU HAVE TALENT? THEN WHAT? YOU HAVE TO FIGURE OUT HOW TO WORK YOUR WAY INSIDE. KEEP UP WITH WHAT'S CAUSING CHAOS IN YOUR OWN FIELD."
>
> Filmmaker John Waters

EVER TRIED. EVER FAILED. NO MATTER. TRY AGAIN. FAIL AGAIN. FAIL BETTER.

Samuel Beckett

FAILURE

• • • • • •

Failure is great. No really, it is. You can't appreciate light without dark. It's important to have regular setbacks, hiccups, and stumbles to give you a sense of reality about where you are and how far you've come. If it were always up, up, up, it would be too smooth, with no cause to reflect on what you'd done so far.

"MISTAKES ARE THE PORTALS OF DISCOVERY."

James Joyce

As soon as something goes wrong or an outcome isn't what you expected, you ask yourself, "Why?" That is a brilliant question that we should all ask more often. That simple three-letter word—*Why?*—forces you to take stock of what you've been doing, how you've been doing it, and what you should change going forward. This is essential to learning and progressing. I know that sounds counterintuitive—to stumble and stop in order to really go forward—but if you constantly and perfectly steam through your goals, you'll be going at 100 mph, never stopping to take in the scenery or look around you.

Fail isn't a negative word. Like the word *work*, it was acknowledged as being a "bad" thing at some point, yet it's the total opposite. We all need failure as much as we need success—you can't have one without the other. It's what you do in those situations when things didn't work out as expected that makes you who you are.

There's nothing more humbling either. Failure makes you take a quick reality check on who you are and who you think you are, and once they're realigned, you're good to go. It's like having an annual checkup on your ego: It keeps things running smoothly.

DON'T TAKE LIFE TOO SERIOUSLY. IT'S NOT LIKE YOU'LL GET OUT ALIVE!

Elbert Hubbard

6
GO FORTH
AND FLY!

Here we are then—the final section. You're nearly ready! We've identified that it's time for something new. We've made a plan. We know how to stand out, and we've got a good idea of the setbacks we might face and how to sidestep them. With all that in our back pocket, it's time for us to face the music—and DO.

Ahead are a few final pointers for staying on track, keeping optimistic, and persevering. This is the exciting part, where we part ways and you fly solo on your journey of awesomeness. It's time for you to step into the cockpit, turn off the autopilot, and take those controls in your hands. Sounds a bit scary, right? It should be, but it feels fantastic at the same time, yes?

Besides, you get to wear a cool little captain's hat, and I get to jump dramatically out of the cargo bay wearing a parachute. Win win!

This is it. It's time. Good luck!

NEW
DESTINATION

CHAP · SEC · PG
00-01-09

BE
HPPY

CHAP · SEC · PG
02-03-28

SAY
YES

CHAP · SEC · PG
03-02-40

MAKE
TIME

CHAP · SEC · PG
05-03-84

BE THE
SUN

04-03-71

GRFT
AND CRFT

06-01-106   CHAP · SEC · PG

CHAP · SEC · PG
03-04-44

TEACH
YOURSELF

BE THE
CHNGE

CHAP · SEC · PG
02·01·23

FIND
BLNCE

CHAP · SEC · PG
05-04-86

GRAFT AND CRAFT

• • • • • • •

Do the work. Put in the hours. I was desperately trying to find a way to gently ease us into this section, but I realized there isn't one. Sorry. And that's exactly the point: there is no sugarcoating. It's now just about hard graft.

Hopefully you're armed with all the tips, pointers, inspirational quotes, resources, and everything in between. But it all comes down to you. You're the one who has to act and put your plan into action. Heck, even if you don't have a plan yet, don't let that hold you back—make it up as you go along. Get into a routine of doing, and you'll soon find that rhythm exhilarating and addictive—the more you do, the more you'll want to do!

It'll get tough. It'll get frustrating. You'll have doubts in your own abilities and the world around you. That's natural. Make sure your balance is in check, and you'll be all good. What you can't do is let that dark side win, because once you give in to the cynicism, well, it's game over, as everything becomes "Why?" instead of "Why not?" and "No" instead of "Yes, and . . ."

As the old saying goes: "Persistence beats resistance, every time!"

It's true: you simply have to persevere through the times when you want to give up. That's a skill in itself—to stay positive and focused—but like all skills, it can be learned and improved. The more positive you are, the easier it is to stay upbeat when things don't go as planned. Nothing worth attaining comes easily.

As human beings, as doers, our actions and creations have the power to make people feel something, to connect, to elicit an emotional response. That is a huge privilege, but one that is available to us all—and that is something well worth grafting for.

YOUR OUTPUT IS THE
NEXT GENERATION'S INPUT

• • • • • •

**As creative beings and people who DO things, we
have the power to make things that will live on—far
beyond their initial outing in the world—to be tiny,
lasting memories in someone's brain. And that's very,
very special.**

How often do you reference other creations? That painting
you love. The album you adore. That novel you've read
twenty-three times. You use these beacons of excellence
and enjoyment to measure against: "No way. Prodigy's Fat
of the Land is not a patch on Jilted Generation," and so on.
They also occupy a very important part of your brain, too,
a place of near-instant recall. I get my mother and father's
birthdays mixed up all the time (Sorry, Mum! Sorry, Dad!),
but I can rap you the entire first verse of Snoop Dogg's "Gin
and Juice"—such is the strong cultural impression it made
on me when I first heard it.

What's most exciting is that all these things that you
hold dear (and recommend constantly to other people,

despite their protests) have been made by another creative being. Someone just like *you* has made this *thing* that you *love*! So why can't you make your contribution, too? Of course there's the talent and hard work of the original creator, but they're still exactly the same as me and you. That thing they made that you love? They probably thought they couldn't do it. They probably thought they didn't have it in them. They probably didn't expect it to happen the way it did.

The point is, they have all the same doubts as we do because that's natural. So now we know that, all we need to do is nurture our own talent and put in the work. Simple, eh?

As well as making memories, the things you output now will be input by the next generation. In six months, six years, or sixty years, a new audience is going to find it, feed off it, change it, twist it, make it their own, and then make something else. You want that input to be the best quality ever, right?

BE CHILDLIKE, NOT CHILDISH

• • • • • •

When we were little, we were encouraged to be curious, to be playful, to explore, and to experiment. We developed our understanding of the world around us from our inputs—those things we exposed ourselves to and experienced. We discovered we shouldn't lick the top of batteries by, yeah, licking the top of batteries. We expressed ourselves by painting and drawing and making a mess. But did you ever once stop and think, "I can't draw; I'm not going to do art today"? Of course you didn't! It was all part of playing and being a child. That wonderful naïveté of learning and doing— regardless of skill level—was all about how it felt.

As we got older, we started to pay attention to that skill level and to hone in on the things we were good at, and we stopped doing the other stuff. Now that's all part of being an adult, sure, but I think it's a crime to ignore those impulses we once had.

Children have this beautiful way of seeing the world— constant questions about every minute detail, unashamed daydreaming about what they see in their mind's eye, and, best of all, a total lack of seeing or understanding barriers. In anything.

Their minds aren't restricted by logic or by social decorum: They just think; they just do. I think we could all do with a little bit more of that in our day-to-day lives.

Imagine if we ran our companies with a little more flexibility, allowing a bit of silliness in every now and then. I'm not advocating a state of pure childlike anarchy where we abandon all structure; I'm suggesting that structure is flexible enough for a little bit of madness, a peppering of fun. Have a space-hopper race in your office at lunch. Bring a trampoline in on the last Friday of every month. They don't have to be big things—you'll be so surprised at the difference in you and your coworkers when you see their faces light up, like they're six years old, when they remember the visceral thrill of simply jumping up and down on a springy surface. And remember: you don't have to be the manager or CEO to suggest these things.

There's also a big difference between being childlike and childish. No one wants to be childish—stubborn, unreasonable, and sometimes selfish—that's the bad part of being young. Being childlike, that's the sweet spot. If you can bring in that childlike naïveté and honesty, that innocence and that joy of seeing the world for what it is, without cynicism or judgement, you'll find yourself smiling a lot more.

Remember: you can't make fun unless you're having fun.

WHAT'S YOUR LEGACY?

• • • • • •

Phew! You made it! Here we are. This is it. The big one. The final piece of advice I can give you. Ready?

Make things that matter so you can leave them behind for others.

That sounds very grand, doesn't it? And it should, because it's such a powerful thing to be able to leave your imprint for others to discover and build on. We can all do it.

I want this statement to make you feel strong and powerful, inspired to do great things, but I also want it to feel realistic. You should make and do things that matter to *you*, that can be left behind—for your dog, your own kids, or the entire human race . . . it's up to you.

Your success and your goals are exactly that: yours. We'd all love to change the world, save the environment, revolutionize education, solve poverty and famine—and for some people that is their goal and their path, and that is their legacy. But just because you want to start an origami business in Warwick because you love the art of folding paper, don't let the comparison of scale make you feel like that's any less impactful. That's your path, and that will be your legacy. We'll all be helping the world collectively if we passionately, positively, and honestly live our lives, pursuing the things that matter to us.

Happiness is a universal currency; a smile is understood the world over. If what you do makes someone grin uncontrollably, then that is a very powerful thing; don't underestimate the value of it. If we could all encourage a little more grinning and a bit less grimacing, then we'd be changing the world in the process, too!

What matters even more is what your legacy should be as a person, what you bring to the world as an individual. Your projects, pursuits, and passions speak volumes, but that's because they're a natural extension of you as a human being. Be kind, be humble, be honest, be open, be supportive, be compassionate, be patient, be engaged, be excited, be dedicated, be true, be absolutely lovely. Be all of these things and more, because that's the real mark of success.

There's a film that I've loved since I was young, but only when I watched it again as an adult did I realize that it features the most inspirational and honest message in its closing scene. Impressive really when you consider it's a 1976 musical gangster film featuring a cast of child actors (with adult singing voices). Yep, you guessed it, *Bugsy Malone*! And it feels like the perfect way to end the book. "Why?" I hear you cry with confusion. Because it feels totally fitting to take our last inspirational words from a film that's full of energy and heart, with the wonderfully silly situation of children masquerading as grown-ups, trying to make their way in the world.

So I'll leave you with this, because never a truer word has been said . . .

YOU GIVE A LITTLE LOVE, AND IT ALL COMES BACK TO YOU.

YOU'RE GONNA BE REMEMBERED FOR THE THINGS THAT YOU SAY AND DO.

RESOURCES

Thanks to the wonder that is the internet, there's a whole ton of inspiration out there, ripe for the picking. Listed here are a few quick hits of inspiration in the form of videos. Head over to your favorite video site and search using the phrase shown below the boxes to find it.

There's a great mix here, some of my personal favorites. From the brutal honesty of Los Angeles tattoo artist Mister Cartoon to the devilish genius of auteur John Waters, it's always fascinating to hear people's stories of how they got to where they are. You can be sure it's never a simple journey. And we can all draw inspiration from that.

Mister Cartoon

🔍 *mister cartoon the run up*

Sir Ken Robinson on nurturing talents

🔍 *sir ken robinson learning revolution*

John Waters keynote speech

🔍 *john waters risd 2015*

John Cleese open and closed mind

🔍 *john cleese on creativity*

Dave Grohl keynote speech

🔍 *dave grohl sxsw 2013*

Jill Bolte Taylor on trusting your feelings

🔍 *jill bolte taylor ted talk*

Lizzie Velasquez on defining yourself

🔍 *lizzie velasquez ted talk*

Sarah Corbett on why shouting quietly gets you heard

🔍 *sarah corbett do lectures*

Akala, rapper and poet, raps the truth

🔍 *akala fire in the booth*

Green is not a creative color (bonus bit of fun)

🔍 *dont hug me im scared 1*

ABOUT THE AUTHOR

Gavin Strange is a senior designer at Aardman Animations, the four-time Academy award-winning studio behind *Shaun the Sheep* and *Wallace & Gromit*. He is a believer in creative side projects and develops his own under the JamFactory moniker. He speaks at conferences around the world including the OFFF festivals, Future. Innovation. Technology. Creativity (FITC), and the WIRED Next Generation conference.

Gavin took an unconventional route to get to where he is today and urges young people to find a fulfilling vocation, to be stimulated and inspired every day.

Gavin lives in Bristol with his wife, Jane, and their son.

@jamfactory | jam-factory.com

THANKS

To my wonderful wife, **Jane**, for her constant love, support, positivity, and encouragement. I wouldn't be able to do what I do without her.

To my mum and dad, **Mick** and **Cindy**, who have always supported me and encouraged me to have a career in the arts, despite me painting the crappiest picture of Vincent van Gogh when I was ten. I hope I'm doing them proud.

To my brother, **Dan**, an inspiration with his kindness, thoughtfulness, intellect, and artistry. He's always teaching me something new and getting me to think about what I already know in a different way.

To **Arnold C. Rockmount**: the king, ruler, muse, and bed monster of our household.

To my **Uncle Kev**, who blew my mind by asking me to question what I was reading in the news, urging me to examine how I was being presented information.

To my family: **the Stranges, the Ryans, the Muddimers, the Tricketts, the Peaces, the Kenneys**. Thank you for the constant support; sorry you're all going to get copies of the book for the next ten Christmases.

To my **friends,** for putting up with my constant sharing of "stuff" all the time. From rants to events, GIFs to graphics. Your tolerance is much appreciated.

To **event organizers** and **attendees**, for giving me your time and the opportunity to share my thoughts and musings on the world, which is a huge honor. Without those talks, there would be no book.

To **Aardman**, for being a place filled with inspiration and wonder. So many amazing individuals doing amazing things; I feel incredibly lucky to be around those people.

To **Jon McGovern**, the stranger I met on a train who offered me my very first talk at the Apple store in Birmingham. I hadn't ever imagined I would have anything worth sharing with others, so this is all down to you.

To all at **Christon Davies**, the design agency that gave me my very first proper job. Thanks for giving a young lad with too much hair gel (!) and questionable music choices a chance to be part of a team.

To **Andy Simpson** at Casino, for encouraging me to make the leap and go freelance.

To **the Do Lectures**, the most mind-blowing, heart-glowing, soul-affirming event I've ever had the good fortune to be a part of. Speaking there led to so many new friends and new inspirations—and this book!

To **Stu** and **Steph**, for bigging me up to David, Claire, and Naomi at Do—none of this would have happened without you. You're the best.

To **Miranda**, the editor and founder of the Do Book Company. These books are all because of you. Thank you for taking a risk on someone who hadn't written a dissertation before, let alone a book. I'm so very proud to be a Do author; thank you for believing in me.

To you, **the reader**. I hope you've enjoyed it. I hope it made you feel something.

Vincent van Gogh, 1992
Gavin Strange
Poster paint on card

Books in the series:

Do Disrupt
Change the status quo. Or become it.
Mark Shayler

Do Grow
Start with 10 simple vegetables.
Alice Holden

Do Story
How to tell your story so the world listens.
Bobette Buster

A percentage of royalties from each
copy sold will go to the DO Lectures,
a workshop series for sharing ideas
and inspiring action.

For more in the DO Books series,
visit **www.chroniclebooks.com.**

To learn more about DO Lectures,
visit **www.thedolectures.com.**